Illustrated

Limericks Of Life

A Bolt Out Of The Blue

By: George T. Jackman

A frisky young squirrel from Pearl Harbor,
(when jumping from fence post to arbor)
touched a live wire bare,
(which stood up his hair)
so he looked like he'd been to a barber!!

A Chipmunks Tale
By: George T. Jackman

Three chipmunks who liked wire (plastic coated),
reclined in their den (bellies bloated).
The wire coatings they'd chewed
left the van's owner stewed,
When his starter repair bill was quoted!!

A Cracked Sewerage Pipe

By: George T. Jackman

Two plumbers (one woman, one man);
A cracked pipe, one floor under "*the can*";
He yelled up "Holy Cow!"
She thought she heard "Now!"
So she flushed, and guess what "*hit the fan*"!

A Down To Earth Girl
"Falsies, Girdles, And Fake Eye Lashes"
By: George T. Jackman

Sometimes women are not what they seem.
They use paints, smelly powders, and creams.
A young man who is wise,
won't be caught by surprise,
when he marries the girl of his dreams!

A Misunderstanding

By: George T. Jackman

The recipe used clearly said,
"Leave room for the cookies to spread."
From the hallway she'd check,
(but not one spread a speck!)
And, she wished she'd made brownies instead!

A Slap On The Wrist

By: George T. Jackman

The defense team presented their list,
(for just a light slap on the wrist!)
The crooked judge smiled
at the unruly child.
The prosecution team left the court pissed!

Acceptance

"We're All In This Boat Together"

By: George T. Jackman

Any "***fruit cake***" (or "***nut case***") you know,
will insure savoir faire where they go.
To be dealt a full deck,
is their "***pain in the neck***".
They just love life from ass to elbow!

Address Unknown

"The Grieving Father…. A Day Late And A Dollar Short"

By: George T. Jackman

He was just off his biweekly "*bender*",
with a small box of fried chicken tenders,
when the money he'd sent,
for his daughter's back rent,
came back red-stamped "Return To Sender".

Angry Blue-Haired Hot Rodder

By: George T. Jackman

It happened at a stoplight blinking;
A bumper sticker got me thinking.
The light had turned green.
She honked and she screamed,
then, flipped me the bird, from her Lincoln!

The Angry Housewife

By: George T. Jackman

"I'd *love* a Greek salad!" he said,
(to his wife with a smiling tipped head.)
But it wasn't *her* job,
to be waitress to Bob!
So she left him a Caesar *instead*.

The Art Collector
By: George T. Jackman

Juanita Montego Montoya
collected rare art works by Goya.
She loaded her mansion,
and then commenced dancin',
while her cleaning man just moaned "Oi, Vi-Yah!"

The "Bad Ass" Student

By: George T. Jackman

Young Jerry "*The Bad Ass*" always cursed.
When confronted, he'd only get worse.
He'd drive teachers insane,
with his language profane,
then, demand his meds from the school nurse!

Barometric Pressure

By: George T. Jackman

A cobbler from cold North Dakota,
had a warm-weather sewing machine motor.
When temperatures dropped,
his chain stitcher stopped.
The stressed man could not meet his quota!

Beatitude
"Blessed Are The Merciful"
By: George T. Jackman

A great shame on American cities,
where the homeless all tent without pity.
The encampments of drugs
are easy pickings for thugs.
While those in power drag their feet in committees!

Bent Out Of Shape

By: George T. Jackman

A director, film crew, and ten actors
(who were trying to record "The X Factor")
saw such push, shove and shake,
(by the 13th retake)
they all needed their own chiropractor!

The Big Bang

By: George T. Jackman

Petey DiPyro was dumb.
He ignited a match with his thumb,
to a candle he found,
on a vacant lot ground.
He exploded beyond kingdom come!

Big Cheese
"Pride Comes Before The Fall"
By: George T. Jackman

The "*Old Man*" thought he was a "*Big Cheese*".
He did what he wanted, when he pleased.
Until two underlings,
dug up past blunderings.
Now he rethinks his own expertize!

Bigoted Boss

By: George T. Jackman

A girl they called "*All Thumbs*" from Wabash,
worked "*under the table*" for hard cash.
The cut crystal ware,
that was placed in her care,
She dropped to the floor with a loud crash!

Black Pots Matter

(a.k.a. Shiny Pan Prejudice)

By: George T. Jackman

The Pot and the Kettle were black.
They lived on Stove's burners out back.
Shiny Pans couldn't stand 'em,
('cause they worked well in tandem!)
And, Cast left the Iron, Stainless lacked!

Blissful Break

By: George T. Jackman

From the river's mouth, out to the sea,
he rowed right where he wanted to be.
He was sick of being bossed;
he'd be free, but not lost;
In his dory, with his oars, and his glee!

Blue-Haired Retirees

By: George T. Jackman

Two "*blue-haired*" old schoolmarms from Dingo,
were dropped off at the Golden Flamingo.
There, they drank bourbon straight
(while discussing their weight)
then were spotted speed walking to bingo!

Cafeteria Culprit

By: George T. Jackman

A vandal-like youth with a marker,
whose sick humor was darker than darker,
scribbled vulgaris thoughts,
in conspicuous spots,
then , withdrew to the hood of his parker!

Celebrating Diversity

By: George T. Jackman

Rob wondered if he was O.K.
All the others in class received "A".
At recess he'd slave
writing "I Will Behave".
while his classmates were outside at play.

Chemical Straight-Jacket
By: George T. Jackman

A yoga instructor and trainer,
was mugged by a psycho restrainer.
To make matters worse,
the pills in her purse,
said Thorazine on the container!

The Christmas Eve Mishap

By: George T. Jackman

A jolly old elf of world fame,
down a chimney in red velour came.
But, wouldn't you know,
the hearth's embers' glow,
set the seat of his trousers aflame.

Class Clown

By: George T. Jackman

Crazy George makes the whole bored class laugh;
(with his side-splitting antics so daft!)
To watch him is a riot;
(if it's funny, he'll try it!)
He's a master at "*plying his craft*"!

Come As You Were

By: George T. Jackman

An actor (with all good intentions)
was surprised when the flyer failed to mention,
that the "Come As You Are,
we will make you a star!"
was a sex-changed transvestite convention!

The Coupon Queen Of Joppa

By: George T. Jackman

Sally Smith was a very smart shopper,
(with the looks of a Vegas show stopper.)
She checked all racks twice,
(left the bad, took the nice)
then cashed out, using coupons and copper!

Courage
"Overcoming Fear And Insecurity"
By: George T. Jackman

From a safe place, where he did abide,
he would take a peek to the outside.
He'd dress incognito,
whenever he did go,
'til he started a group called Gay Pride!

Cutting Corners

By: George T. Jackman

Young Billy Bean had a bad habit.
He'd race through his chores like a rabbit!
When his mother would check,
she'd proclaim, "What The Heck?",
"You've left dirt in the corners *DAGNABIT*!!!"

Dancing With Don Ho

By: George T. Jackman

A Midwestern weight-watcher named Beulah,
had a passion for dancing the hula.
In between Don Ho hits,
her silk muumuu split,
when she grabbed a Diet Coke from the cooler!

Deja View

By: George T. Jackman

A French artifacts digger named Irma,
o'er the mountainous jungles of Burma,
ran out of gas
through the Pagodas Pass,
and crash landed on strange Terra Firma!"

Desperados Waiting For The Perdue Train

By: George T. Jackman

Most "*Free Ranging*" chickens aren't fat.
They just eat "*on the go*" (and that's that!)
Their favorite places
are the "*wide open spaces*",
where they roam with their guns, masks, and hats!

The Diabetic Coma

By: George T. Jackman

When a case of cannoli arrived,
into the box grandpa dived.
Until later that night,
he ate bite after bite.
It's a wonder the old man survived!

The Dismal Attitude

By: George T. Jackman

In a town very close to the sea,
dwelt a man, who caressed misery.
"Life Sucks, Then You Die!"
Was his hourly cry;
his true self-fulfilled prophesy!

The Preventative Stressor
"Down The Road"
By: George T. Jackman

To prevent "***Down The Road***" pain reactions,
his young dentist advised an extraction.
But to tell you the truth,
Bud felt too "***Long In The Tooth***",
and would sooner be laid out in traction!

The Drag Race
"There's A New Kid In Town"
By: George T. Jackman

In a small town in East Indiana,
young Fred was the new *"Top Banana"*!
Old Karl was unseated,
when his *"Rod"* overheated,
and young Fred stole his girlfriend, Rosanna.

First Impressions
"Don't Judge A Book By Its Cover"
By: George T. Jackman

"He was up to no good!" they all said.
"Take a look at the hair on his head."
"His high boots and tight jeans
are like none that we've seen!
He should be more like us folks, instead!"

Focus Drugs

By: George T. Jackman

In a Southern New Hampshire High School,
quiet classes and labs were the rule.
Prescribed "Focus Drugs"
(With smiles and with hugs)
turned kids into zombies who drooled!

The Frenzied Mad Shopper

By: George T. Jackman

At a waiting line **Big Bargain Day**,
in her place, a **Type "A"** wouldn't stay.
Though the cop tried to stop her,
the frenzied mad shopper,
just charged through the doors anyway!!

Fuel Injection
By: George T. Jackman

A slowing ball player from Knox,
played softball, with other *"old jocks"*.
When trying his steals,
his sox fell to his heels.
So they filled his legs with Botox!

The Gambler
By: George T. Jackman

A poker-faced gambler out West,
always played his cards **close to his vest**.
Up his sleeve he would hold
cards, so **he'd never fold**.
But his **ace in the hole** trick was best!

The Gluttonous Drag Queen

By: George T. Jackman

A drag queen (who they called Regina)
stuffed her mouth full of sausage and wiener.
At the barbecue bake,
she took all she could take.
Then, hoped that nobody had seen her!

Gratitude
"I Think, Therefore I Exist"
By: George T. Jackman

Two cavemen, just *"chewing the fat"*,
as sparks flew 'round the fire where they sat,
talked about strife,
in their primitive life,
then, thanked heaven, for where they were at!

Greed
"Rip-Off At The Pharmacy"
By: George T. Jackman

Leaving sick and tired "***pinned to the walls***",
Our government sputters and stalls.
The high costs of our meds
should be lower, instead,
Big Pharma "***has us all by the balls***"!

Hairdo Gone Wrong

By: George T. Jackman

From her neck hung a "Hands Free" type mirror,
(that reflected her curling work clearer).
But each curl that she gripped,
caused the mirror to slip,
'til her hairdo looked queerer and queerer!

The Haldol Zombie

By: George T. Jackman

There once was a boy sent to school,
whose behaviors would break every rule.
His intent was so bad,
the SPEDS drugged the poor lad,
'til, alas, he did nothing but drool!

Hallway Resolution

By: George T. Jackman

A teacher (whose patience was tapped)
With a stun gun haphazardly zapped
Some miscreant kids
For the things that they did
While their head sets boomed out "*gangsta rap*"!

The High Blood Pressured Shopaholic

By: George T. Jackman

A young, self-proclaimed shopaholic,
(whose baby was plagued with the colic)
had to rush from the floor,
of the T.J. Maxx store,
when her blood pressure soared diastolic!

Hoopla
By: George T. Jackman

Our basketball players at school
are lanky and tall (as a rule!)
They jump up and down,
take shots from "downtown",
"beat buzzers", "steal games", and "act cool"!

Hyperactive Habit

By: George T. Jackman

Since his first sip of sugar-filled cola
(from the rear of a double twin stroller)
mood swings bizarre,
for his course became par,
so they labeled him Chronic Bipolar!

Hyperactive Sid

By: George T. Jackman

Sid just couldn't sit in his seat still.
He had cravings for sweets and weak will.
In school caf they'd serve
drinks that bothered his nerves,
and off-set his Adderall pill.

Ironclad

By: George T. Jackman

Miguel Marinara Montoya
suffered real maritime paranoia.
At the piers and the floats,
where others brought boats,
Miguel docked his salvaged destroyer!

The Joy Ride

By: George T. Jackman

"Stop It!" She cried (through her laughter.)
But he pushed, even harder and faster.
'Til what seemed a great thrill,
midway down the hill,
turned from fun , to a certain disaster!

The Junk Food Junkie

By: George T. Jackman

An "Old Timer" (outside T.J. Maxx)
waited calm in his car (quite relaxed).
While his wife shopped the store,
(for more bargains galore)
he sat feasting on junk food-type snacks!

Kindness Through Actions
"A Person Of Integrity"
By: George T. Jackman

A lawyer who made time to spare,
helped to hurdle a publishing snare.
Her nickname was Kate,
And she "*opened the gate*".
Her kind acts were extraordinaire!

King Of The Castle

By: George T. Jackman

He argued with his future "ex",
over charge cards, commitment, and sex.
He went out to his chores,
She locked windows and doors,
and left him in the dog house with Rex!

The Love Lorne Worm

By: George T. Jackman

'Neath a craggy old bent Gala tree,
a worm (from his apple) could see,
his dream mate in clover
(just three fruit trees over)
was a cross-dressing **_he_**, not a she!

Mistaken Identity

By: George T. Jackman

A seagull, from high in the sky,
saw a meal in the sand wiggle by.
He dove to the spot,
and bit what he caught,
while a sunbather screamed out "Oh My!"

Moderation

By: George T. Jackman

Over the Falls at Niagara,
in a barrel, went a stiff from Kiagga.
He thought of the fact,
that there was no turning back,
and, he'd taken too many Viagra!

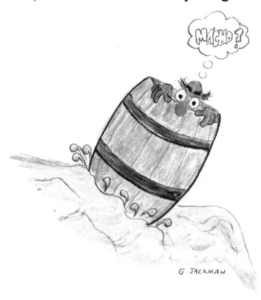

G. JACKMAN

The Multi-Tasking Dog Walker

By: George T. Jackman

Up a tree, on a limb, under bower,
sat a long-haired unruly chihuahua.
His owner (with leash)
cell-phoned the police,
took pics, and sent texts, for an hour!

Painting The Town
"Someone Has To Put Their Foot Down"
By: George T. Jackman

She was having good times, running 'round!
She was flirting and "*painting the town*".
When the cat is away,
those mice will sure play!
It was high time he "*put his foot down*".

The Little Leader

"It's Not The Size Of The Dog In The Fight, It's The Size Of The Fight In The Dog"

By: George T. Jackman

Little Pee Wee was small for his age.
From the start he could take "***center stage***".
When a leader was needed,
the big boys conceded;
his mischief-making ideas were the rage!

Phonic Pressure

By: George T. Jackman

A non-reader who entered grade K,
fell behind the 8 ball his first day.
Classmates (he could tell)
could already read well,
while he couldn't the alphabet say!

The Phony Phone Call

By: George T. Jackman

A young man (whose real name was Doug)
would call school saying he had the bug!
In a voice (like his mother),
he'd fake a sneeze smother,
then hang up, and smile (feeling smug!)

The Phys. Ed. Skipper

By: George T. Jackman

A kid from the big "Baby Boom",
hated to shower and groom.
He'd skip his gym classes
(with forged doctor's passes).
Then "get stoned" in the school's boiler room!

Poop-Scoopin' Flaw

By: George T. Jackman

Our Poop-Scoopin' Law has a flaw;
it mocks every Health Code it's for.
Because some "*in the loop*",
plastic-bag their pet's poop,
then throw it back down with guffaw!

Power And Control
By: George T. Jackman

A rude student, so darn "***non-compliant***",
was, by no means, a scholarly giant.
In his classrooms he'd ply
a Modus Operandi
That turned teachers "***oppositional defiant***"!

The Pride Of The Nepts

By: George T. Jackman

In our town was a Fife & Drum Band,
which showcased its cymbals clash man.
His antics and dance
(planned well in advance)
left thrilled spectators clapping their hands.

Rebel Without A Cause
"A Bad Influence"
By: George T. Jackman

He was always in trouble at school;
a *"Bad Apple"*, who broke every rule!
If he had his druthers,
he'd influence others,
to do all things he does to *"Be Cool"*.

G. JACKMAN

The Room With A View

By: George T. Jackman

The day was a wonderful Easter,
where the Matriarch smiled at her vista.
But all who sat frowned,
when her dress slacks fell down,
'cause the old lady'd worked off her keister!

Rubber Necking
"Old Habits Are Hard To Break"

He had controlled it as long as he could,
(his **rubber necking** in the neighborhood!)
No matter how hard he tried it,
his true nature denied it.
He couldn't mind his own business as he should!

School Graffiti
By: George T. Jackman

A boy (with obnoxious behaviors)
marked lunch tables with foul engravures.
The custodians fumed
as they sprayed, scrubbed and broomed,
while the SPED's fantasized they'd be saviors!

The School Recess

By: George T. Jackman

In a school yard (at recess and play)
he was offered some free "Mary J".
Though at first he denied it,
being pressured, he tried it,
and was stoned for the rest of the day!

Seeing The Light
By: George T. Jackman

A young lad (who knew right from the start)
that for Language and Math, he'd no heart,
felt like a champ,
manufacturing his lamp,
and thanked God he was spatially smart!

Story Teller

By: George T. Jackman

A student with dark, curly locks,
avoided the gym and the "jocks".
He loved books instead,
and, the jokes that he read,
he retold to his friends on the blocks!

Stretching The Truth

By: George T. Jackman

Old carpenter Pat "Stretch" Mahoney,
was tall, lean, and strong (albeit boney.)
At the pub he would tell
tales (fictitious as hell)
'til the patrons would yell, "*THAT'S BALOGNA*!!!"

Sugar High

By: Jackman George T. Jackman

A lad with "Attention Dysfunction",
was prescribed (without any compunction)
a strange hocus pocus,
(to help him to focus)
And, to offset high sugar consumption!

The Sugar Shack

By: George T. Jackman

\

At a quaint sugar shack named "Au Sucre",
hung a slogan (a real party pooper!)
"You Are What You Eat
From Your Head To your Feet".
Food for thought, while you lick your three scooper!!

Sweet Revenge

By: George T. Jackman

A skunk on a neighborhood street,
searching trash cans , for something to eat,
when attacked by a dog,
sprayed a perfumed stink fog,
and the canine ran off in retreat!

Sweet Tooth
"A Good Invitation To The Blues"
By: George T. Jackman

He had a "**sweet tooth**" (it was said).
Eating candy went right to his head!
The sugars he craved,
changed how he behaved.
And, a good boy turned "**hyper**", instead!

Take That Hat Off

By: George T. Jackman

A student in the foyer who chatted
with friends was brow-beaten and battered,
by a teacher who said,
"Take that hat off your head!"
"We have school rules to follow!" he added.

Telecaster Master

By: George T. Jackman

The son hammered riffs clear and fast,
(fumbling slightly through "Classical Gas.")
On his new Telecaster,
He played louder and faster;
(dad's bona fide ***pain in the ass***!!!)

The Broken New Year's Resolution

By: George T. Jackman

She was determined to work out each day;
do Pilates, eat tofu, and pray.
But then (just by chance)
she was seen in large pants
at the ***All You Can Eat Brunch Buffett!***

The Devil's Advocate

"Mister Nosey"

By: George T. Jackman

Mister Nosey liked nosing around.
He could "*dig up dirt*"all over town!
One sniff to his snout,
would wipe out any doubt,
that if you'd done something wrong, you'd be found!

The Impression

By: George T. Jackman

Leroy "The High Diver" Sewell,
impressing some girls (like a fool)
sprung high from the board,
just to find, as he soared,
the water had been drained from the pool!

The Machinist Lunch

By: George T. Jackman

A machinist named Teddy McTag,
(whose production, 'round noon time, showed lag!)
Would go to the pub,
for some drinks and a sub,
then return to work "*half in the bag*".

The Prankster
By: George T. Jackman

Young Randy (from South Pensacola),
Drank nothing but warm Coca Cola.
His prankster friend, Ed,
Slipped him iced-tea, instead,
And thought "He won't know shit from Shinola!"

The Slippery Banana Peel

By: George T. Jackman

Her nickname was "Sure-Footed" Jackson.
She was always ahead of the action.
Until one day and place,
a felon she chased,
threw a fruit peel, that led to her traction!

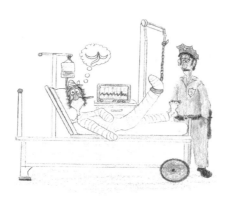

The Stunned Opposition

By: George T. Jackman

A young Coe Brown center named Josh,
between two huge defenders, was squashed.
He grabbed the rebound,
then slam-dunked it down!
While the Portsmouth fans gasped "Oh My Gosh!"

There Goes
The Neighborhood
By: George T. Jackman

There was an old man from Calcutta,
who had lived a long life (without clutter).
His days and nights spent
(In pure Karma content)
until Walmart became an abutter!

Too Old, Too Soon, Too Fast
"Perfect Practice Makes Perfect"
By: George T. Jackman

An old timer just learning to fiddle,
was confused by a curious riddle.
Slow waltzes were fine,
but the jigs' 6/8 time,
would get him so lost in the middle!

Tuba Woobah

By: George T. Jackman

In our school there's a band member who
blows a mean Sousaphone ("right on Cue!")
With his John Phillip zest,
he plays scales with one breath,
and, makes music without turning blue!

Turkey Neck Bud

"Grow Old Along With Me, The best Is Yet To Be"
By: George T. Jackman

He was fat, he was bald, he was smugly.
When he looked at the girls, he'd get snuggly.
But, "Old Turkey Neck" Bud,
was a self-proclaimed stud,
and, to tell you the truth, he was ugly!

The Two-Timing Jerk

"Foolish Is The Man Who Breaks His Marriage Vows"

By: George T. Jackman

It was down at the Golden Banana,
he was seen, "*in a lip-lock*" with Anna.
This "*two-timing*" jerk,
drove his good wife berserk.
She trashed their home, then left for Montana!

Un American Activities

By: George T. Jackman

Oil companies driven by greed,
take twenty times more than they need;
set record high prices;
get tax-exempt slices;
and in Swiss banks, interest guaranteed!

Uncontrolled

By: George T. Jackman

A young woman (whose name I'll withhold)
was high-strung and demanding (I'm told).
She went totally berserk,
and assaulted the clerk,
when her layaway Valium had been sold!"

Unexpected

By: George T. Jackman

Fresh from a Ku Klux Klan henchin'
a man (with a thirst he kept quenchin')
had a bad stroke of luck,
when he boarded a truck,
headed straight to a Black Power Convention!

Unhealthy Eater

By: George T. Jackman

There once was a fellow named Peter,
whose wife was a very poor eater.
For her noon lunch-time break, she'd
eat whipped cream-topped cake, then
drink down a coke by the liter!

What Pooper Scooper Law?

By: George T. Jackman

Two elderly on their daily sojourn,
(trying their best to stay healthy and firm,)
were seen tiptoeing through
a fresh minefield of poo,
thanking God folks can't walk Pachyderms!

Yard Sales
"One Man's Trash Is Another Man's Treasure"
By: George T. Jackman

They turn their old cars on two wheels,
(just to find the great buys and best deals.)
They speed into lines,
of cars following signs,
to the yard sales of bargains and steals!

You Are What You Eat

By: George T. Jackman

A woman (who loved fettuccine)
couldn't fit into last year's bikini.
All the pasta she ate,
more than tripled her weight,
(leaving her in dire need of a genie!!)

CPSIA information can be obtained
at www.ICGtesting.com
Printed in the USA
LVHW080903081221
705586LV00003BA/47